# Lewis Hamilton
## Racing Beyond Limits

Graymalkin Creative

# The Fastest Man in Formula One

Lewis Hamilton is one of the greatest racing drivers in history. He has broken records, won seven Formula One World Championships, and inspired millions of fans around the world. But his journey to the top wasn't easy.

Lewis was the first black driver in Formula One. He faced racism, financial struggles, and pressure from all sides. Still, he never gave up. He believed in his dream and worked harder than anyone else to reach it.

This is the story of a boy from England who became a global champion - not just on the racetrack, but also in life.

# Early Life in Stevenage

Lewis Carl Davidson Hamilton was born on January 7, 1985, in Stevenage, England. His mother, Carmen, is white British. His father, Anthony, is of Grenadian descent.

Lewis lived with his mother until he was 12, then moved in with his father, stepmother Linda, and half-brother Nicolas, who was born with cerebral palsy.

From a young age, Lewis loved speed. He raced remote-controlled cars and often beat adults in competitions. He was also quiet and focused - traits that would help him become a great driver.

# A Kart and a Dream

When Lewis was six, his dad bought him a go-kart. It wasn't fancy, but Lewis drove it like a pro. Anthony promised to support his son's racing dream as long as he worked hard in school.

Anthony worked up to four jobs at once, including IT work and cleaning, to pay for karting. Despite facing racism and unfair treatment, Lewis stayed focused. He won karting championships across the UK and Europe.

At age 10, Lewis approached McLaren team boss Ron Dennis and said, "I want to race for you one day." Ron smiled and told him to call in nine years.

# Climbing the Ranks

Just three years after that meeting, McLaren signed Lewis to their young driver program. He began racing in bigger and faster cars.

He won in Formula Renault, then in Formula 3, and finally in GP2. In 2006, Lewis won the GP2 championship in his rookie season.

It was clear he was ready for the biggest stage of all: Formula One.

# Formula One Debut

In 2007, Lewis joined McLaren in Formula One, becoming the first black driver in the sport's history.

He finished third in his very first race and came within one point of winning the world championship in his rookie season.

In 2008, at age 23, Lewis made history by becoming the youngest World Champion at the time, and the first black driver to earn the title.

# A Bold Move to Mercedes

In 2013, Lewis made a surprising move. He left McLaren to join Mercedes, a team that hadn't been winning.

Many thought he was making a mistake. But Lewis believed in the team's vision and in himself.

With Mercedes, he won six more world championships and broke records for most wins, most podiums, and most pole positions. By 2020, he had tied the great Michael Schumacher with seven world titles.

# Using His Voice

Lewis spoke up against racism and stood for fairness and equality. He became a strong voice in Formula One and beyond, championing many important social causes.

He also supported efforts to make motorsports more diverse and inclusive.

Outside of racing, he became vegan, supported animal rights, and pushed for a greener planet.

In 2021, Lewis was knighted, earning the title "Sir Lewis Hamilton" for his incredible achievements and activism.

# Setbacks and Strength

Even champions face tough times. In 2021, Lewis lost the world championship on the final lap of the last race. It was one of the closest finishes in history.

In the years that followed, he didn't win another world title and even went a full season without a single race win. But Lewis didn't give up. He kept training, kept racing, and kept striving to improve.

Through every challenge, he showed the world that true champions never stop pushing forward.

# A New Chapter with Ferrari

In 2025, Lewis joined Ferrari, the most legendary team in Formula One. He wanted a new challenge, and fans around the world cheered.

At age 40, instead of retiring, he chose to chase one more dream: helping Ferrari return to glory.

The red suit, the passion, the fire - Lewis was ready.

# Still I Rise

Lewis Hamilton has shown the world that greatness isn't about where you start. It's about how far you're willing to go.

He broke barriers, used his voice, and chased his dreams all the way to the top. Through victories and setbacks, he kept moving forward with courage and determination.

His favorite words, borrowed from a famous Maya Angelou poem, remind us all to stay strong and keep going: "Still I Rise."

"Don't listen to anybody that tells you you can't achieve something extremely impossible. Speak it into existence. You've got to work for it, you've got to chase it, and you've got to never give up and never doubt yourself."

**Lewis Hamilton**

Printed in Dunstable, United Kingdom

73694424R00016